*Thrifty*RICH

*Thrifty*RICH
A Thrift Diva's Journey to Joyful Abundance

By Margie Freeman DeWoskin

CHAPEL HILL
PRESS, INC.

ISBN 1-59715-009-6
Library of Congress Catalog Number 2005932021

Printed in the United States of America
First Printing

The Japanese iris on the cover represents thriftyRICH abundance and prosperity. It is one of many flowers that multiplied from a friend's generous sharing of her resources after she had received them from another friend. My bucket of bulbs, planted in five groups, have multiplied and will again be divided with other friends.

Finding the Abundance and Prospering!

Beth Landi, creative writer and knowledge seeker, helped organize my journaling pages and her vision kept *Thrifty*RICH in motion.

David B. Freeman contributed generously many hours of editorial time.

Brad Freeman, well-known book artist, generously donated his time and talents in seeing ThriftyRICH to completion. He is the photographer of the cover. He is also my brother.

Rob DeWoskin, avid scientist and mentor to many, as well as my husband, edited and guided me to the finish.

Abundant buckets of gratitude to them!

Table of Contents

Preface and Dedication

There have been times in my life when I have had money, property, and many possessions, and times when I've had very little. But I have always been thrifty and lived well. As the years have gone by, I've learned that living well means more than having money. It means being *Thrifty*RICH no matter how favorable the Fates are to me at any given time. You can be *Thrifty*RICH too!

I remember my most desperate time of "being without," after a bankruptcy, the loss of my home, and a divorce. I had no choice but to depend on my own resources to survive. The holiday season that year had none of the opulence under the tree with which my two daughters and I were familiar, but we still found a way to share hand-made gifts, gifts from a thrift store, gifts in "good as new" condition.

Those times of little money challenged my creativity and my ability to muster all of the resources I could to meet my family's needs. I learned about the importance of being grateful for the resources I did have: healthy parents who offered shelter and nurture, helping hands and day care from social agencies, food stamps, school lunch programs, and the support and loving-kindness of my family, my community, and friends. I learned new ways to use, to reuse, and to recycle everything in sight! I discovered the wealth of affordable goods in thrift stores and how much fun it was to find "treasures" that met our needs: furnishings for our home; school clothes, toys, and books for my daughters. We made it our game. "Goody," my oldest daughter would say when it was time to shop. "I love thrift stores!"

By learning to make choices that matched my resources and to manage these resources to meet our needs, I was able to move forward and have all of the abundance I needed. I had become *Thrifty*RICH. By the time I married my second husband, eight years after starting over, I had earned a master's degree, had a professional career, and had saved enough money to pay my half of a down-payment on our first home together. I was proud of what I had accomplished.

Now my two daughters, Anneliesa and Dona, have their B.A. and M.S.W. degrees, respectively. I continue to have fun finding thrifty treasures for my friends and family, and especially for our new grandson, David Joaquin Augusto Aguayo. I dedicate this book to my husband, Rob, our daughters, their husbands, our grandchildren, and my parents, Thomas Parker Freeman and Laurie Freeman.

As your life unfolds, may the stories and lessons in this book help guide you toward gratefulness, a recognition of the abundance in the world, and the joyful life of being *Thrifty*RICH.

Margie Freeman DeWoskin
Durham, North Carolina

How to use this book

Let me offer a few suggestions on how to use this book. Read a page or two each day. Take some time after each section to get in touch with your thoughts and feelings. If you like, you can use the space at the end of each section to write some of these thoughts as well as changes or actions you might like to take. This practice can lead to concrete changes. Writing in the book also will make this experience more personal for you. It also makes this your workbook. The affirming rituals and ideas will easily become an integral part of your day, assisting you on a positive path toward the abundance and joy of a *Thrifty*RICH life.

What it means to be *Thrifty*RICH

It always seems so simple, once we learn how

"I love your cashmere sweater," Terri said as she admired my "new" outfit. "Where did you get it?"

"Where else?" I replied. "A thrift store."

Terri's eyes widened. "That looks brand new!"

"It is," I laughed. "And my silk top, gold bracelet, and coat are also from a thrift."

"Oh, Margie, how do you find these treasures?"

"It's easy and fun," I assured her, as I tell all my friends who marvel at my constantly changing wardrobe of good quality clothing. There is an abundance of perfectly good outfits at thrift stores. All kinds of life's hidden treasures can be found at thrift stores, sometimes brand new once you know how to find them.

Being *Thrifty*Rich, though, is much more than finding a good value at a thrift store. Being *Thrifty*Rich is about being aware of the abundance that is available to us in so many areas of our lives. It is about making choices that match our resources, and choosing resources that meet our needs. *Thrifty*Rich is an awareness of what we do have, sharing that generously, and being good stewards of ourselves *and* our resources.

*Thrifty*RICH *is a journey into financial serenity, gratitude, and generosity*

After months of marveling at my inexpensive new clothes and accessories, Terri finally joined me in a thrift store outing. We walked into one of my favorite thrifts, and immediately I found a batik blouse. Terri found a mug that she wanted. We had a blast, and her awareness of abundance had begun!

It was difficult for Terri's family to have new expensive clothes or jewelry and, growing up, she often felt that she was missing out. As a working adult, she would hold off as long she could, but sooner or later, she felt the need to treat herself to something special, usually something more than she could afford. So out came the credit card, and more debt, leading ultimately to an even worse feeling of not having enough, of running on empty.

Thrifting has changed that feeling for Terri. Now when I see her, she'll say, "I never really understood what you meant when you would talk about financial serenity, of having faith that my needs would be met and that there really is enough. But since I've been shopping at the thrift for everything from my nearly new microwave oven to my 14k gold necklace, jeans, and my many cashmere sweaters, I now know, first hand, that my material needs can be met without a huge credit card bill. You helped me find the freedom to enjoy what I have without worrying about piling on more debt. Best of all, my creative energy now goes into thrifting instead of endless dreaming about having more and more money so I could really spend mega-bucks. My old high school friends can't believe how well I live without spending a lot." Now instead of richly spending and skimpily living, she is Thrifty Spending and Richly Living!"

Thrift and rich defined

A quick search of popular dictionaries resulted in the following definitions for "thrift" and "rich."

Thrift A *noun*, originating from Middle English, perhaps from an Old Norse word for prosperity "*thrīfask*" meaning to thrive:
1. The sensible and cautious management of money and goods in order to waste as little as possible and obtain maximum value
2. A thriving state, good husbandry, economical management in regard to property
3. Increase of worldly goods
4. Success and advance in the acquisition of property
5. Vigorous growth of living things, such as plants

In other words, being thrifty means to acquire property and money and to manage money and property well so that it grows (vigorously) and you prosper.

Rich An *adjective*, originating from prehistoric Germanic words borrowed from Celtic words akin to Old Irish *rí* (genitive *ríg*) meaning king.
1. Having abundant possessions and especially material wealth
2. Having high value or necessary or valuable qualities
3. Magnificently impressive, sumptuous

4. Vivid and deep in color (a rich red), full and mellow in tone and quality (a rich voice), strong in fragrance (rich perfumes)

5. Abundant in materials—yielding great quantities of anything valuable

6. Amply supplied

Being *rich* means having affluence, wealth and abundance; an ample, copious, fruitful, plentiful, sumptuous, precious, generous, and spicy supply of whatever immaterial or material goods or qualities you need.

What does it take to be both thrifty AND rich? To be only thrifty without feeling rich is to place too much of an emphasis on frugality and parsimony. To use wealth without being thrifty is to live without economy or good management of resources. To be both thrifty and rich, to be *Thrifty*RICH is to manage whatever resources are available to you while maintaining an inner awareness and feeling of abundance.

Putting it all together—the full definition of *Thrifty*Rich:

- An awareness of and how to find the abundance in your life
- Thrifty management of the resources available to you
- Learning how much is enough for you and sharing generously with others
- An ability to replace feelings of emptiness with feelings of gratitude
- A dedication to a sense of well-being and joyfulness in sharing life's abundance

~ *Thoughts, Feelings, Actions* ~

~ *Thoughts, Feelings, Actions* ~

Recognizing abundance

Too much stuff to love

Two-year-old Aurora Brynn was stunned upon entering my room lined with ceiling-to-floor shelves of toys, games, and puzzles.

"Too much stuff," she exclaimed!

She went to one familiar toy, a Fisher-Price radio, and quickly took it out of the room. Wise enough to realize she could not play with them all, she chose one recognizable piece and moved it away from the confusion of too many toys.

Have we forgotten our limitations? Do we have too many toys, too much stuff to love? Look around your space. Take an inventory of the things that fill your life and your space. One day I noticed that my creative writing table was so full of "inspirational objects" that my attention was being pulled from my writing and constantly drawn to all the items that were meant to inspire my writing: the box with the inscription "Sense and Serenity," the healthy happy picture of me—age 53—in a frame that says "Prosperity," the jar that says "Ready Ideas," my Asian stone and sand garden waiting for me to arrange, my beautiful pottery, books on investments, books with blank pages, my journaling pages, and even recipes! Too much stuff had transformed a working space—my writing table—to an altar of my inspirational objects. No work was getting done because the "inspirational" objects were a distracting clutter. Too much stuff on my altar!

Do you have too much stuff on your shelves, too much stuff in your closets, in your attic or garage or on your to-do list? Do you have too much stuff to enjoy? And even in the midst of all of your stuff, do you find yourself wanting more? Are you always wanting more storage, more closets, more space to hold things you feel you need? Would that solve the problem of not having enough?

Too much stuff to maintain

Are you smothered in maintenance projects? Are these projects a good use of your creative energy? Finding, accumulating, caring for, storing, repairing, maintaining, and managing stuff—is that what you are living for? If every time you pass an object you think, "I really should dust that, or fix that, or rearrange that," then that item is taking your energy and taking your time—time you may want to spend on other thoughts or pursuits. Every little thing requires some attention and space and maintenance. Holding on to too much stuff becomes hoarding and gets in the way of spending time in purposeful living.

The Depression brought a whole new set of traumas and responses for many families

Did you have family members who saved—maybe hoarded—who were young during the 1930s, the decade of The Great Depression? Their generation developed a profound sense of insecurity when the country experienced this debilitating scarcity of resources. They responded by accumulating goods and money for future rainy days. This was a wise response to a time when food and other daily requirements were often difficult to find. Many people developed a feeling of "never having enough" and unwittingly passed that insecurity from generation to generation. Children are sensitive to the habits and feelings of their parents. Did your parents save rubber bands, bags, jars, and old objects in their attics, basements, and closets "just in case" they might need them because they remembered a time of "not having" and the trauma of scarcity? Some people feel an urgency to accumulate — money or goods or anything — in order to lessen their fears of not having the necessities.

Early patterns and family values establish our financial habits and attitudes

Examine the messages received from your family's financial management behavior. What was felt, seen and heard early in life becomes firmly fixed in patterns and habits that can profoundly influence our adult behavior. There are many ways to examine, re-examine, or maybe discover for the first time, past events that determine today's behavior. What is the history of your family's financial values and behavior? How has wealth in your family changed over the previous two or three generations?

Living above and beyond our means

What happens when the trauma of scarcity meets the cornucopia of today's marketplace? In the latter half of the twentieth century, living above and beyond our means became possible and, for the average person, even the expectation. This trend continues into the twenty-first century. It wasn't until the 1900s that "regular folks" could accumulate an abundance of stuff. Before the twentieth century, only landowners and the upper classes had the means to accumulate wealth and to pass that wealth on to their heirs. In the early 1900s, manufacturing practices and rapidly growing cities led to opportunities for the "common folk" to gain and pass on wealth.

Today, aggressive advertising plays on our fears of scarcity while availability and easy financing of products encourage excessive accumulation. We have more stuff than ever before. Credit cards encourage instant gratification and postpone the need to acquire funds before acquiring goods. Feelings of "not enough" and spending more in an attempt to create "enough" are the norm for our culture. A *Thrifty*RICH lifestyle may seem impossible to imagine because our cultural practice is to have the rich life without thrift behavior.

~ *Thoughts, Feelings, Actions* ~

_____

_____

_____

_____

Matching resources to needs

When our values today do not fit the
financial models from the past

What can we do when we begin to realize that our financial behaviors are relics from the past? If excessive hoarding or excessive debt was a family pattern, and you do not want to live that way, you can change. Look at your core issues around spending to identify patterns that cause trouble. Do you hoard or spend excessively?

We don't have to stay stuck in behaviors from the past. We can choose to start our own traditions, habits, and attitudes that make sense in today's world for our financial resources. Destructive patterns from early conditioning are powerful, but having knowledge and wisdom about financial resources is also powerful. It does take willingness and openness to change. It does take awareness and honesty about our deficiencies, our real needs, and our resources to meet those needs. It can be done!

The part we play

First we must see the part we play in our outcomes. For example, Janice has no money for the tax bill that is due on her car. She has no concept of saving from one month to the next for the bills that will arrive in six months or a year from now. Her resources seem never to be enough for her needs. There always seems to be some unexpected emergency, some outside reason for her being in debt. She never examines her patterns of spending; her expenses are always beyond her income. She understands how to do simple math, but she never uses it to her advantage. She loves to eat out with her friend. Dinners out—$8.95, add drinks at $2.95 each, plus tip, plus tax, and multiply by two—and $30 is spent. That is enough money for groceries for four days! Janice never makes the connection between her behavior and the constant need for money. What is her part in these choices and why is it so destructive to blame circumstances for bad outcomes? What happens as her debt increases and more needs are unmet in the future?

If we never see our part in creating our circumstances, how can we ever change?

~ *Thoughts, Feelings, Actions* ~

_____

_____

_____

_____

_____

_____

_____

_____

The seed must shatter its bounds to create the new plant

We can free ourselves from the bonds of bad patterns that lead to bad outcomes. Yes, we can create new, positive habits. With vigorous honesty about the part we play in creating bad outcomes and with a willingness to learn, we can become *Thrifty*RICH. Change, even unwelcome change, often brings growth. Change cultivated into opportunity brings creativity in new ways of being and living. The seed must shatter its shell to create the new plant. If the seed stayed within the safe bounds of its shell, it would never germinate. It would rot. If we stay the same, feeling safe even if our patterns are destructive, what new life are we missing? How much of ourselves are we losing to decay?

Knowing yourself and the path that brought you here

An unexamined life eventually leads to difficult living, difficult for you and for others. Examine how you arrived at where you are today. Begin to see how choices made or not made took you down a certain path, led you to your present situation, whether living is full of debt and unfilled needs or debt-free with adequate savings and a feeling of abundance and wealth.

Our life is created by daily choices, choices that we make consciously or unconsciously. As we become aware of how the choices we made in the past led to our present reality, we begin to move toward a path that will lead to wiser choices for our future financial, physical, emotional, and spiritual well-being.

Desiring more than our resources can support is a cause of suffering. Choosing to buy what we can't afford, not our limited resources, causes our suffering. Choosing, seeking, and purchasing what we can't afford financially or energetically cause great suffering and damage to our mind, body, and spirit. "More" is the addiction of our times and culture. Our economy thrives on more. The marketplace urges us to spend more, buy more, use more, have more, want more. We must resist the advertisements that try to convince us that we are "less" unless we have more. Resist this!

Be purposeful with what you bring into your world. Each purchase, each item you bring into your life, takes energy from you. Our stuff always requires looking after—cleaning it, moving it, storing it, using it. It continues to require more of our time, more of our energy and, of course, more of our money. Match your daily choices for your accumulations or commitments with the personal resources available to you. These resources (time, energy, money, health) expand and contract on a daily basis. When you stay within the boundaries of your resources, you will not over commit and go into debt. Over commitment leads to physical and emotional bankruptcy. When we owe more money, time, and energy than we can reasonably afford, the price we pay in worry, sleepless nights, stress, and strain drains our Total Being.

~ *Thoughts, Feelings, Actions* ~

_____

_____

_____

_____

_____

Financial serenity is about faith

Financial serenity is about having the faith that you have the resources that you need. It is also about wise action, about acceptance when you can do no more. Financial serenity is about faith in your ability to match your resources with your needs. When you know what "enough" is for you and have faith in your ability to match your resources with your needs, you will be free from the unending cycle of unnecessary accumulation. Faith is also trust in the abundance of the universe and in the creativity and resources that your higher power will provide to you. Faith, however, is not blind trust that no matter what you do all will turn out well; rather it is a trust that if you try your best and seek out the path that is right for you, you will receive the help and resources that you need.

The opposite of faith is fear. Fear of economic insecurity will leave us as we practice a *Thrifty*RICH lifestyle. Financial serenity is the promise that has come true.

Open yourself to the possibilities of meeting your needs

I need transportation. I need food. I may desire to own a Lexus or a BMW, but I have many options for transportation. I may desire lobster bisque and filet mignon, but beans and rice and salad make a delicious and nutritious meal. I need clothing. I may feel that only a cashmere jacket from a department store will fill that need, but a thrift store has racks of barely used and even new name brand and fashionable clothes, including that cashmere jacket. All for a fraction of the original price! Satisfying our needs is possible if we explore alternative ways to meet those needs.

~ *Thoughts, Feelings, Actions* ~

_____

_____

_____

_____

_____

_____

_____

_____

_____

_____

_____

_____

_____

_____

_____

_____

_____

_____

_____

_____

_____

_____

_____

Be grateful to be *Thrifty*RICH

Why more stuff does not fill the emptiness

Many of us try to solve a spiritual problem with a material solution. We seek material possessions to fill the void from unmet spiritual needs, and no amount of things ever seems to fill that void. Emptiness of spirit cries out to be filled but will never be sated with material things. If our identity, our sense of self worth, is based upon how much we spend and own, then we will never be able to spend enough to maintain a high level of self-esteem. No amount of spending and acquiring will fill that bottomless pit of increasing self-doubt and loneliness. Accumulating more things does not satisfy, because the solution to filling emptiness is not material. That hole in our soul is filled with what we can't see or buy or hoard or earn or put on layaway. That hole lies within and needs to be filled from within. Finding gratitude for what we have now is how we start.

Can we ever be grateful for more if we're not grateful for a little?

A search for more rather than experiencing the pleasure of enough is the hallmark of addiction. Always wanting the whole cheesecake after a taste, the whole bottle after a glass, more lovers, more chocolate, more jewels, more of anything is the "never enough" of addiction.

"More" is the disease of our consumer culture. All addictions and abuses are about wanting more. To unduly want more of any good thing turns our pleasure into an obsession that eventually grows so demanding that it works against us. It can destroy us.

~ *Thoughts, Feelings, Actions* ~

_____
_____
_____
_____
_____
_____
_____
_____
_____
_____
_____
_____
_____
_____
_____
_____
_____

Joy is peace dancing. Peace is joy resting.

Gratitude has no wings. Gratitude gives rest from the flitting around of overdoing and wanting. Gratitude is pausing to be grateful for the richness of this moment. Life is both the resting and the dancing. Both doing and being become partners in a celebration of life.

Gratitude begins with acknowledging all that we have

Gratitude begins with the conscious choice to acknowledge what we have and what is available to us. Living in a democracy gives freedoms and privileges that allow sharing the collective wealth. With little personal wealth, all share in the wealth of a country that has public schools, extensive libraries, national, state, and city parks, highways, public programs, and thrift stores. To live in a culture of abundance and wealth gives us a huge advantage even if we have less income and fewer personal resources than we would like.

What are the abundances in my life, the privileges and resources available to me?

To attain an attitude of gratitude, begin by making a list that acknowledges all that you already have—a list that begins with this moment. Write down ways that you benefit from living in an affluent democratic society, from your social connections, your family, your work, the leisure activities available to you, the right to own your own home, and access to health care. Write about your appreciation for your special joys like autumn leaves, fresh air and water, peace within, and a grateful heart.

～ *My gratefulness list* ～

_____

_____

_____

_____

_____

_____

_____

_____

_____

_____

_____

_____

_____

_____

_____

_____

_____

_____

_____

_____

_____

_____

_____

_____

Be giving to be *Thrifty*RICH

A clinched hand can never receive

A grateful attitude nurtures a generous spirit. As I remember all for which I am grateful, I know that I have enough. And having enough, I know there is plenty to share. A generous hand is born of a grateful heart. A clinched hand can never receive. An open hand, ready to give, is also ready to receive.

Giving starts a cycle of generosity and a flowing of abundance back and forth, sometimes quickly and sometimes slowly, but it will always happen if we are receptive.

Money begets money, smiles beget smiles,
good deeds multiply and grow

Generosity feeds on generosity. The seeds of gratitude grow the flowers of generosity. A generous person is secure in the knowledge of abundance. Generous people have the assurance that their needs will be met and that there is plenty to share. There is a gracious plenty.

*Thrifty*RICH *is about spreading the*
wealth and sharing the joy

*Thrifty*RICH is about generosity of spirit, spreading the wealth and sharing the joy! We can all give generously and receive abundantly when we are *Thrifty*RICH. In thrift stores, folks are having a good time because they are spending a little, not a fortune. If someone seems to be looking for a certain item that I've found, I joyfully show it to them. And I've had people want me—beg me—to buy something just because it looks like it's my size. We want others to share the joys of the treasure hunt!

After all, there's a lot more where that came from. Each treasure is a chance to be generous to yourself and to someone else. You will always be rich when you have a generous spirit and a *Thrifty*RICH heart!

There is an unintentional consequence when you give freely

Giving generously creates an energy of giving. A willingness to share opens the river of giving as things flow more freely. We aren't the owners. We are only the loaners and borrowers of stuff. I have a basket on "loan" to a coworker to use in a photo of his new baby. I'll borrow it back someday for my grandbabies. A gift of a puzzle to my dental hygienist was enthusiastically received. Then a magazine I had been seeking was a gift back to me. The intention of generosity is not reciprocity; but reciprocity is often the unintentional consequence. When you give freely—so shall you receive.

The same day the basket became a gift,
I found four more at a thrift store!

Letting go of some stuff frees us to enjoy what we have and to be assured that there is more, without accumulating more. I enjoyed a pretty autumn basket for several weeks and then gave that basket away to my coworker Nacy to enjoy. Filled with fun snack treats, it made a special fall/Halloween treat. A few days later, a bag of sweet potatoes, my favorite fall food, with a note from Nacy was waiting for me on my desk. I didn't expect sweet potatoes in return, but there they were. Giving generates generosity. And the same day the basket was given away as a gift, I found four more at a thrift store!

Gathering and letting go, a need to balance the flow

We spend much of our early years gathering stuff. Then there comes a time of letting it go, a need to balance the flow. Building a nest with things you love, you may realize that you have way too much. It's time to let go. It's time to pass on the excess and share with those in the gathering stage.

Open and clear — get your stuff down to the essence of what matters most to you

How can we open and clear rather than fill, close, and clutter? First, remind yourself of your values, then start practicing the process of deciding what goes, what stays, what to buy, as well as what to sell or share. With every choice you make, your values will become clearer and your stuff will reflect those values more and more. Remember, your possessions can support your values instead of being distractions or intruders that steal from your life your precious time, energy, and attention.

Freedom from the maintenance of stuff enables choices about what to let in. Empty spaces allow expansive choices, openness to new opportunity. Look at any item that you add and see the energy, time, and upkeep that it will take. Get your stuff down to the essence of what matters most to you.

~ Thoughts, Feelings, Actions ~

Start with sharing the surplus

Start with reducing what you already have. Give, loan, or sell your surplus stuff to others. I had 40 houseplants, 30 of which found new homes as gifts to my plantless friends. The same happened to the surplus of outfits crowding my closets. Each item of clothing that is not truly useful or beautiful should find its way to some other receptive body. Share and dispense. I could never enjoy what I had when I was spending too much time, money, and energy on what I didn't really want, couldn't use or, worst of all, didn't even need or like. Start with sharing the surplus. Don't settle for what isn't the best match for you and your values.

Enjoy the process of giving generously to those who can appreciate it! A nearly new sweater can have a new life with someone else! Who needs it? Who wants it? Incomplete projects can become someone else's hobby. A basket can become a birthday gift with pampering items. Recycle and share the wealth generously. Give freely what you have so freely gathered. Pass it on.

Being present may be the best present

You give to others also by sharing your energy and your time. Listening, caring, being present with another are the ultimate gifts to that person and to you. As one connects, one is connected.

Kindness is another generous gift. Kindness is what I want from people...gentle treatment. Kind thoughts and gentle exchanges in a sometimes harsh, hurried, and thoughtless world are a gift and a blessing. Kind actions offer a welcome haven.

Do we think too highly of our ability to know whom to serve?

Am I always able to judge when someone is suffering or deserving of my gifts? Many suffer in silence; others may not seem deserving. It is better to acknowledge that all people may be suffering and all are deserving. Suffering comes to those who seem to have much. Also people who can't express appreciation can still be deserving of our gifts. As we meet people along our path, we choose who shall receive our gifts. If we think too highly of our ability to know best when and whom to serve, we may ignore someone truly in need. If we are always searching for a more worthy recipient, we might lose the opportunity to share with someone who is close by and needs our gifts. Maybe those in our path were put there for a reason. Maybe we are their best (maybe their only) hope for today.

In generosity, we allow forgiveness of others and of ourselves. We forgive the slights, the unkind word, the shortcomings of others, and hope the same from them. We are only able to change our own attitudes, actions, and responses. We cannot change others. But we can be generous in our forgiveness.

A forgiving heart is a generous heart. A generous heart rejoices in another's good fortune and helps others less fortunate. Good fortunes come in a healthy life, in loving relationships, and in our attitude of gratitude.

Let yourself be surrounded by a cocoon of interdependence, connections, and closeness

Helping others builds trust that others will be there when we need help. Remember that good feeling, that special glow, when someone thanked you for helping them in some way? It works both ways! Let someone else experience the glow of helping next time you have a task that could use some more brains, more hands, more heart. We weren't meant to live, work, or play in isolation. Join hands and circle round the next event. Let yourself be surrounded by a cocoon of gossamer threads, each lightly connecting around your being, and extend these threads to others creating interdependence, connections, and closeness. Giving allows us also to receive help. When we give, we build community and relationships that grow and nurture. Coming together for "thanks" we create "Thanks-giving."

If we are not generous with those closest to us, what is the point?

Don't forget to be generous with those closest to you. If we can't be generous with them, what is the point? Many charitable causes are worthy of our support. Does it make sense, though, to be generous to worthy charities and not be generous to those closest to us: our children, our friends, our families? Do those closest to you take second place to the neediest? Will they learn that they have to be needy to be worthy of your attention and your love? Enjoy and share financial resources with charitable causes, and with friends and family in adventures, trips, vacations, and with gifts that recognize their value. Should we wait until we die for our wealth to be shared with our family and friends—after the fears of not having enough are finally no longer a concern? What is the point of saving if the savings are never enjoyed? What is the point of passing savings on to heirs if we are not sharing generously with them while we and they are alive?

An affirmation

I am worthy of the wealth I've accumulated and worthy of the joy it can bring to me and others. I want to spend it wisely in a balance that is *Thrifty*RICH in enjoyment and pleasure.

~ *Thoughts, Feelings, Actions* ~

Be well to be *Thrifty*RICH

The spirit of generosity ... starts with being generous and good to yourself

The spirit of generosity is pervasive and contagious. And it starts with being generous and good to yourself. Let life be your bowl full of cherries—enjoy some now, and freeze some for later. Too much waiting to enjoy the fruits of your labor and the fruit goes bad! Be a partner in the journey; enjoy the path along the way, while balancing enjoyment in the day with mindfulness of the future. Being generous with yourself frees you to be generous with others. The time and energy spent for self-caring is nurturing and so creates more energy to care for others. If self-caring is neglected, a dangerous pattern of parsimony is created. Withholding and stinginess of caring behavior, as well as jealousy of others' ability to be self-caring, may occur. Do for yourself what you wish for others.

A ThriftyRICH lifestyle creates a sense of well-being

A sense of well-being—physically, financially, socially, mentally, and spiritually—is what being healthy really means. Being well and staying well is a lifelong process toward wholeness and the prevention of disease and illness. In a MacArthur Foundation

Study of Aging in America, titled "Successful Aging,"[1] Drs. John W. Rowe and Robert L. Kahn define successful aging as "the ability to maintain three key behaviors or characteristics:

1. Low risk of disease and disease-related disability;
2. High mental and physical function; and
3. Active engagement with life."

A *Thrifty*RICH lifestyle creates a greater sense of well-being and saves megabucks in our medical budget—an area that grows exponentially as we age. To age successfully, we must thriftily manage our resources for the prevention of disease and for continued well-being so that less is spent on medicines, hospitals, and body repair. Successful aging includes exercise, proper diet, smoking secession, treatment for any abuses of drugs or alcohol, massage, movement and dance classes, spa vacations, and fitness club memberships. The time you take for self-caring now is money in the bank later. This self-caring applies to all aspects of your health—physical, mental, social, spiritual, and financial. Remember, your well-being is the source of your most important resource—your Total Self.

> *"As long as I'm moving, they can't bury me!"*
>
> —Corinna Wicker (at age 82), Sanford, North Carolina

It was my privilege to know Corinna Wicker through the Senior Community Service Employment Program. She was the oldest worker in the program in Lee County. Despite having

(FOOTNOTES)

[1] Rowe, John W., Kahn, Robert L. (1998). *Successful Aging* New York, Pantheon Books

an aggressive form of cancer, she kept working 20 hours a week and refused to have me or anyone carry her mail to the post office as long as she was able. She kept moving until the last month of her life.

Two thrifty and easy ways to stay healthy are to drink six to eight glasses of water a day and to keep moving—walk, bike, swim, jog, dance, and build strength. Life is movement. Movement, internally and externally, keeps us going! Bodily movement and activity and connections with people, friends, confidantes, and fellow travelers all help us stay healthy and enjoying life. Active involvement in causes and projects keeps a body in motion.

Work your body daily through cardiovascular exercise, strength building, and movement to increase flexibility. Take a yoga or exercise class; gentle stretching is wonderful. Exercise in water if land movement is difficult. Move your body. Exercise 'til the cows come home! Find a fun movement and do it! Walk a lot. Walk everywhere. Dance! Swim! Jump rope! Run! Play!

~ *My exercise program* ~

_____

_____

_____

_____

_____

_____

_____

_____

Your body and mind and spirit need
daily attention and quality time

Self-caring is multi-faceted and purposeful. Attention to your values and what matters to you is a major part of investing in yourself. Eat balanced and healthy meals. Nourish your mind with good literature. Join a book club and participate in enriching conversations with friends and family. This will lead to and stimulate thinking. Feed yourself good thoughts. Keep learning throughout your life. Creating healthy images of your self-caring and visualizing where you want to be will get you there.

When always on the path of Doing
we leave little time for Being

Are you always "Doing"? Are you always busy with busy-ness, taking care of chores and maintenance? Always doing leaves little time and energy for being. Quiet times will help calm the body and slow the pace of our too busy lives and allow for spiritual connection. Noise, clamor, and busy-ness are not conducive to spiritual connections. The lines of communication open as we clear the clutter and slow the pace. Take the time for your life; the chores will still be there when you return!

Values clarification helps us know ourselves

Taking care of yourself means knowing your values. Ask, "Am I working and living in order to use my financial resources to create a life that reflects my values, my larger goals, and my purpose in life?"

By creating a vision for your life that satisfies your values, you begin to see how your financial resources can be used to accomplish those goals and dreams. But financial resources are only part of your assets. Take a good inventory of all of your gifts and talents that can be put to good use for both your benefit and the world's. How are your time, money, and energy used to fulfill your life's mission?

~ *My mission statement* ~

_____

_____

_____

_____

_____

_____

_____

_____

_____

_____

_____

_____

_____

_____

_____

_____

_____

_____

_____

_____

*"Get behind your favorite cause or
advocacy issue and keep pushing."*

—Ann Johnson, North Carolina advocate for the aging

You can make a difference in this world. Identify your values, preferences, strengths, and limitations. How does your calendar reflect where you spend your time? What do your checkbook and credit card statements say about where you spend your money? The dollars and time spent are a reflection of your life. Where do you put your life's energy, time, and effort? Do you feel balanced? Would you like to spend more time and money in any one area? What can you change to make that happen? What distractions, other people's expectations, addictive behavior, or unhealthy patterns and self-imposed barriers are stopping you from self-realization, from having the life you want? Give yourself time and take time for yourself to do the things you want to do and to be the person you want to be. No one else can do it for you.

~ *My causes* ~

_____

_____

_____

_____

_____

_____

_____

_____

_____

_____

_____

_____

Seek help from others: friends and family,
professionals, your higher power, nature

Knowing ourselves, we know how to ask for help. You are your best resource, but sometimes you need to ask for outside help. Ask for help. Do you have a network, a community of friends, a faith family, coworkers with whom you can talk, neighbors you can trust, relatives, fellow travelers, or a higher power to which you can turn?

Seek professional help if you are overwhelmed and confused about how to become healthier. Seek a support group to help stop your addictive behavior: alcohol, drugs, food, people, spending. Self-help groups abound. Look around! Call a mental health center if you feel unable to understand your thoughts. Look in the yellow pages, newspapers, weekly news magazines, the Internet, and the library. Ask! Seek out the healthiest people you know and ask how they do it. What help did that person receive?

Connect with a higher power—as you define it—as your partner in all that you do. We aren't on this journey alone. We only have to ask for help, and turn on the power—the higher power.

Communing with nature is centering and rejuvenating; make it a daily practice. Be outdoors and appreciate something in your natural world today!

~ My human and spiritual resources ~

_____

_____

_____

_____

_____

_____

_____

_____

_____

_____

_____

_____

_____

_____

_____

_____

_____

_____

Seek out those wishing to build rather than destroy the richness in living

Say "no" to destructive forces that would erode your self. Relationships with destructive, dysfunctional, critical, and/or sarcastic people can undermine your healthy, positive thinking. Resist and fill your life with mutually beneficial, healthy, growth-seeking, and nurturing people who are on a path of wholeness. Show loving kindness to those in your path, even the "toxic" few, but seek out those wishing to build rather than destroy the richness in living. Construct the path of healthy wellness and follow the journey of a happy destiny. Are you ready for it? Or is the comfortable, dysfunctional crowd still OK with you? Create your best Self: physically, mentally, socially, financially, and spiritually.

Taking care of yourself means using your gifts

Use your skills, your talents, your life experiences, your sense of survival, your network of friends and relatives, your community, and your higher power. All the resources within your realm of imagination and even those you have yet to discover are yours to tap. Tap the greatness of your abilities.

Your talents are unique. Hear what you are yearning to do! See the way for naturally using your time. When you allow yourself to be free to explore, to what are you drawn? Gathering stones to polish, planting seeds for harvest, seeking treasure among the tossed, cooking abundantly the harvest of autumn, seeking, inventing, writing, fixing, dancing, drawing, listening, searching, accepting, nourishing.

How many ideas for inventions and entrepreneurial endeavors have come from one person's imagination and creativity? Who thought of yoga? Who created the wheel? Dreamed up the idea of blowing glass? Wrote the first word? Recited the first poem or sang the first song? Listen to that still small voice of creativity within you, and don't let the clamor of outside or inside nay-sayers dissuade! The voice of invention is persistent! Help it be heard within you.

~ My talents and ways I can enjoy them ~

_____

_____

_____

_____

_____

_____

_____

_____

_____

_____

_____

_____

_____

_____

_____

_____

Being ThriftyRICH is also about what we don't do

We don't fill our bodies with junk food or beverages that do damage, add fat, or raise cholesterol. Junk food and beverages create sluggishness and immobility, unhealthiness, and unhappiness. We don't fill our minds with negativity, resentments toward others, or harbored anger from past grievances. We don't hold fearful or hostile or unforgiving thoughts for wrongs done. We don't allow toxic folks—those who would do verbal and physical harm—to take up space in our lives. We choose not to let them live "rent free" in our heads.

We don't accept dysfunction or disease as the "way it is." Instead, we seek treatment and knowledge, therapy, support, and understanding. The Serenity Prayer can guide and direct:

Grant me
the serenity to accept the things I cannot change,
the courage to change the things I can,
and the wisdom to know the difference.

~ *Things I cannot change* ~

_____

_____

_____

_____

_____

_____

_____

_____

_____

_____

_____

_____

_____

_____

～ *Things I can change* ～

_____

_____

_____

_____

_____

_____

_____

_____

_____

_____

_____

_____

_____

_____

_____

_____

～ *Self-care checklist* ～

____ I honor my values.

____ I honor my own expansive creative energies.

____ I am with people who encourage and celebrate me and my special gifts.

____ I choose environments and settings that nurture my growth in home, work, and leisure.

___ I nourish my body with good food and drink.

___ I keep my body in motion, strengthening and stretching.

___ I exercise my mind with new wonderment and discoveries and adventures.

___ I give myself breathing space and time to enjoy my life— appreciating beauty, pausing in gratitude, and connecting with people and nature and a higher power.

~ *Ways I am good to myself* ~

_____

_____

_____

_____

_____

_____

_____

_____

_____

_____

_____

_____

_____

_____

_____

_____

~ *Thoughts, Feelings, Actions* ~

*Thrifty*RICH financial how-to's

We find financial serenity by following a *Thrifty*RICH path: making choices that match our resources and using resources to meet our true needs. We arrive at financial serenity by sharing, spending smartly, saving wisely, accepting our whole being and the things we cannot change. Here are some practical tips and how-to's.

Live debt-free — the more we spend,
the more we spin out of control

The average credit card debt is five figures: $10,000, $20,000, $30,000 or more. Drowning in debt is not an exaggerated phrase. For many, it is a hidden condition. And like most addictions, overspending makes our lives feel unmanageable and out of control. Just like a compulsive overeater, gambler, or alcoholic, we keep reaching for our "drug of choice."

The more we spend, the more we spin out of control. What do you need to do if huge debt has become unmanageable? Start by asking for help through your local consumer credit counseling or debtors anonymous organization. Get a plan to get rid of debt and a plan to stay debt free. Make interest; never pay interest!

Save money … pay yourself first

A long-standing financial dictate is to save 10 percent of your income. Saving 10 percent is harder at some stages of life than others, but decide what would be a doable percentage for you for now, and save that amount. Methods of saving money range from using a cookie jar to using brokerage services, but always pay yourself first the percent upon which you have decided before making any other purchases. Pre-taxed funds taken out of a paycheck each month work well. When saving for a special event or item to be purchased within a six-month period, it's best to save additional money in an easy access savings account. Each month, set aside until the goal is reached. If you think you have no cushion, no "extra" to save, look at your money gobblers and leakages. The next section will help you with these problems.

Slay money monsters that gobble your resources

Where are the leaks in your ability to channel your resources? What is slipping through the holes in your pocket? What is being lost unconsciously while you aren't paying attention? The largest money monsters are the ones that convince us to seek continuous pleasure through constant and instant gratification. They gobble our money without our conscious awareness. What are these monsters? The most serious are the major addictions:

_____ junk food
_____ cigarettes
✓ daily/multiple trips to coffee shops
✓ alcohol and other drugs
_____ gambling
✓ compulsive shopping.

~ *What are your monsters?* ~

_____

_____

_____

_____

_____

_____

_____

_____

_____

_____

_____

_____

_____

_____

_____

_____

_____

_____

_____

Stop the unnecessary leakage of your resources

What are the little things that result in not having the resources to get what you truly value? What drains your spare change? Is it worth stopping some of these leakages to have your resources available for what you truly value? For example, is the soft drink or candy vending machine worth the dollar twice a day? Small purchases add up. If you think about being *Thrifty*RICH first, before buying small items, you save many dollars a year. That $1 twice a day adds up to $2 a day. At five times a week, it means $20. Over the course of a year, it adds up to a whopping $1040. Yikes! You could bring your own healthier snack of fruit or crackers or whatever and take a trip with the $$$ you save!

We can't eliminate the expense of food, but we can lessen the costs

Food is one of the categories for which we cannot lower the expense by reusing or buying used. We can ride with others, and we can wear our same clothes over and over. Each day, however, we need a certain amount of new nourishment—food and beverage. Once we are living independently, we have to provide that for ourselves. Fortunately, in the United States, the government has established several programs for people who do not have the financial resources to meet all their nutritional needs. If you are in need and can qualify, take advantage of programs like food stamps, WIC, senior centers with congregate nutrition sites, school children's lunches and breakfasts, Meals on Wheels, and homeless shelters. I've taken advantage of most of these resources during various stages of my life and so can you. If you find yourself in the fortunate position of not qualifying for any of these and you need to provide your own nourishment, here are some *Thrifty*RICH tips:

- Keep eating-out to a minimum. The cost of a single fast food meal can be the cost of a whole week's worth of groceries.
- Order water rather than drinks in restaurants.
- Take your lunch to work; it's much cheaper than eating out.
- Do the math on meals, snacks, and daily beverages. Bring your own from home.

- Avoid buying individual servings in containers. If you eat 32 ounces of yogurt a week, why buy eight-ounce containers? Get a reusable container and scoop out your daily serving.
- Buy in bulk or quantity. Twelve individual rolls of toilet paper are twice the price of a 12-pack. You know you're going to need it. Buy bulk cereal, beans, and grains at much lower costs than individually packaged or canned goods.
- Create your own baked goods. Biscuit mix is only flour, leavening, salt, and shortening. Cake mixes are the same with flavorings and sugar. You are paying for the pretty pictures on the box.
- Create your own soup, salad dressings, and sauces. Specialty sauces are usually made from readily available spices and are very high-priced.
- Never waste. Use up stuff before it goes bad. The "special of the day" is a creative dish you can make from what you have in abundance. Whatever looks like it should be used needs to go into that next salad, soup, or dessert. Be creative.
- Eat what is seasonal. Buy only vegetables and fruits that are in season or on special. Plan your meals after you know the discounts for the week.
- Buy larger amounts of perishables at better prices per ounce or per pound and freeze in family-size portions.
- Use store discount cards and coupons for groceries, other products, and services.
- Store brand items are almost always a better deal than brand names, sometimes even with a coupon for the

brand name. Don't be lured into thinking a brand name is better. It usually isn't.

- Read the labels. Check price per quantity and cost per ounce. A larger package may have less product inside!
- Cook in bulk and freeze for later when you might be pressed for time or creativity.
- Bring your own popcorn and snacks to the theater.
- Be a smart, savvy shopper. Don't be lured by pretty packages and pictures. Impulse buys are fun, but they are usually not good values.
- Cook creatively and enjoy your own cooking. Lick and grin!
- Share that creativity with neighbors, friends, or relatives. Bring friends and family together for communal meals.

Small purchases can add up to large bills... Pay bills on time!

As you rethink your purchases and your habits, take a look at how your credit bill adds up. Do you constantly have late fees or end up paying interest for purchases that don't really meet your values? Do your small habits or instant gratification purchases add up to big spending? Always pay bills on time. If you never seem to be able to, look at those smaller items and impulse buys to see if they are the big gobblers of your resources.

Reuse and make your own

Opportunities abound to make your own household products inexpensively. Recipes for homemade cleaners, fresheners, or repellents from common and inexpensive ingredients are easily found in columns like "Ask Heloise" or in books at the local library or on the Internet. It's much cheaper to make your own, and often they work just as well (sometimes better).

Most items can be used again, even if not for the same purpose. My father saves string, medicine containers, soda bottles,—most anything for now and future uses. For example, he'll cut plastic soda bottles in half to place over his figs on the fig tree to protect them from bees (works great!). I save grocery bags—paper and plastic—and use them for my kitchen trash can liners. Why pay for plastic "trash bags"? Luncheon carry-out containers make great containers for "meals on wheels" for friends or relatives.

Sometimes reusing is also a way of reducing the amount of stuff you bring into your life. I like to collect baskets, but I'll also use them as gifts or packaging for gifts or as storage containers for other things, like bathroom toiletries, stationery, toys, and games. That way I can enjoy my hobby and not have too much inventory (or should I say clutter) at the same time. Teach your children…break the cycle

Teach your children about money. We learn from the habits, patterns, and addictions of our parents and elders. If you have bad patterns, break the cycle and teach your children the *Thrifty*RICH lifestyle. Be purposeful about helping them practice responsibility with money. Give them an allowance so they, too, can learn about choices with financial resources. Teach them delayed gratification, and teach them how to live well without spending a lot. Children who don't learn thrift at home may have money problems all their life. If we didn't learn from our parents how to be *Thrifty*RICH, we owe it to ourselves and our kids to break the cycle!

~ Thoughts, Feelings, Actions ~

_____

_____

_____

_____

_____

_____

_____

_____

_____

_____

_____

_____

_____

_____

_____

_____

_____

_____

_____

_____

_____

_____

The wise spender knows to plan for the unexpect

None of us knows what will be in the future. Spending up to our current income is a dangerous denial that the unexpected can happen. The wise spender knows to plan for the unexpected. The "unexpected" is to be expected. Incomes can suddenly and unexpectedly cease; expenses can increase. The best way to insure always having enough is to save, reserve, put aside, and invest some of what you make. If your income continues to increase without any breaks and your expenses decrease, consider yourself one of the rare and lucky ones.

Insurance… is it unnecessary or the best protection against worst case scenarios?

Insurance protects us from unexpected losses that can wipe out years of savings. Insurance can also provide a security cushion that frees up resources that would otherwise have to be saved for future crises. How much insurance to buy and what kind depend upon how much savings and valuables you feel you need and must, therefore, protect. Exploring how you feel about insurance is another good way to learn about your values. Do you want to over insure so that everything you own is covered, maybe even so you could make money in a crisis? Or do you deny that anything catastrophic will ever happen to you and so feel, why bother? You may rarely benefit from an insurance claim, but like the rest of your *Thrifty*RICH lifestyle, be willing to pay to insure only what you value in your life— nothing more, nothing less.

Invest for the long term while you save

Most millionaires are not obviously wealthy. Their money isn't spent ostentatiously. The book *The Millionaire Next Door* by Thomas J. Stanley and William D. Danko talks about ordinary folks in middle-class neighborhoods who have accumulated wealth. In the late 1990s, with 20 percent and higher returns being made in the stock market, the millionaires next door saw tremendous increases in their investments. In a downturn, these same folks may only be worth half a million, but they live in such a way that it will accumulate again to the million dollar mark. Why? They invest. They know the power of compound interest. They are savers not spenders. They invest in companies according to their value and growth potential, so their wealth will also grow. They know how to find buying opportunities and follow the truth that consistent investment cost-averaging is the key to becoming "the millionaire next door."

*The greatest wealth is inward satisfaction, with a Thrifty*RICH *lifestyle*

How do everyday people who accumulate wealth do it? They don't wear or drive their wealth. They don't wear high-priced, full-priced clothing. They know their car is one of the worst investments. They buy only what they can pay for (new or pre-owned) and avoid paying the additional financing costs on an asset that is losing value. Many drive the same cars for many years, avoiding the loss of paying for new cars every two or three years. Their first homes were probably modest, and they built equity and resisted the temptation to move too quickly into fancier or larger homes (taking on more debt) until they could comfortably afford to do so.

Practicing delayed gratification has increased their savings and will provide the resources they will need for many years to come. Simply put, their money isn't spent to impress others or to bolster their self-esteem. Their wealth isn't directed toward outward show. Their greatest wealth is inward satisfaction, with a *Thrifty*RICH lifestyle.

Never pay full price…comparison shop…sales are everywhere

*Thrifty*RICH means rarely paying full price. There are almost always better deals to be made. Comparison shop for absolutely everything, from car repairs to physicians, from credit to home entertainment. Most companies and providers are willing to meet or beat their competitors' prices.

Get your timing right for the better deals and reap modest to tremendous savings

Some months are famous for certain sales. January is the month for "white sales" for linens, sheets, and towels. End-of-season sales start way before the end of the season. Does winter end in February? No, but spring clothes begin to appear then, and winter clothes become deeply discounted. If you buy your winter sports equipment and clothes in February, you will still have a month to use them. Often you can find specialty stores that have good quality used items at half the original prices, or even more than half at the end of the season. Even jewelry has its discount season. Handcrafted items frequently have discounts twice a year. If your timing is right, you can scope out better deals and reap modest to tremendous savings!

Always check to see if you can get what
you want used before buying new

Think of all the stuff that is available in stores other than in a retail store. All the gifts you'll ever need to give, many of the clothes you want, household items like dishes, utensils, furniture and appliances, books, jewelry, tools, CDs, toys can be found used or sometimes new in thrift and second-hand shops, at yard sales, and swap meets. Thrift stores even have blank celebration cards at five or ten cents each to accompany your thrift gifts. You can create your own sentiment or create your own card and save $$ per card.

You can often find new stuff for less at large discount stores. Shop around and call for the lowest prices. Use coupons. Grocery stores now have their own cards for standard discounts, so get their cards. Clip coupons from advertising flyers or newspapers for double off, and watch for the occasional triple off or unlimited coupons that can add up to lots of money. Savings can be as high as 20 percent. Twenty percent saved is like making a 20 percent higher salary. And you can be creative with savings on coupon promotions. A cereal you wouldn't usually eat may be great as snack mixed with nuts for that company potluck. Be creative and experiment with new things when you can get a good deal!

Reap the benefits of benefits

We are blessed to live in a culture of plenty and abundance. We have wealth, and we share wealth. We have programs, services, and benefits because of legislation and political action and money to spend. Some would say "not enough" benefits for the abundance of our country, yet many programs aren't fully utilized. The National Council on the Aging Inc. has a Web site (www.benefitscheckup.com) with information on available benefits. Check with your Council on Aging or Area Agency on Aging for other services for older adults. Local libraries abound with information and provide free access to the Internet. One of the best, yet underutilized, resources is your local telephone book's listings of community service organizations and information resources on community services.

Some of the best things in life are free — Enjoy them

Nature puts on fantastic shows: sunrise and sunset, dew on spider webs, daffodils in spring. There are nature trails through protected lands, Carolina blue skies, evergreen trees, and sassy spring wild lilies along the Eno River Trail where I live. What is nature showing in your neighborhood? Many, many activities are free for your entertainment:

Going to the library and reading magazines and books
Street fairs..........Flea markets
Museums (free or by donation)
Parks
A warm bubble bath
Taking walks
Watching children play and playing with them
Growing plants, flowers, and veggies (almost free)
Singing, dancing, and moving your body
Smiling, laughing, and making love

~ *Fun-for-free things I like to do* ~

Intake and output

We have things coming into our lives—the intake. And we have things going out of our lives—the output. Your output is another person's intake just as your intake was their output.

When you find that your home is starting to look like a thrift store, it's time to do some serious output. What clothes have accumulated that you don't wear? The newer, most stylish can go to consignment shops. What those shops do not sell will be given to homeless shelters, welfare-to-work women, and nonprofit organizations.

Simplify by swapping or giving to friends. I have a book club group that has an annual dress-up and swap party. We give each other jewelry, hiking clothes, and dress clothes. Then the unclaimed clothes go to women in a work training program. My favorite yoga pants and top came from that swap, and my favorite picture is of a happy, healthy me dancing in them.

Let a family celebration or holiday exchange be a recycle event. Kids can have fun learning how to shop at yard sales or thrift stores, and with the bargains available, they can afford to give as generously as adult spenders. Many laughs and much appreciation have come from these celebrations, and the givers aren't left in debt. Thrifting provides a chance to give back. If you received something you don't really like from someone, you now have another opportunity to give back to the thrift store.

Redo and renew and refresh

Why not pass on what is no longer suitable, fashionable, or likeable? Offer that stuff to others to redo or renew. How often have we heard that someone's trash is someone else's treasure? One can often find unfinished projects in thrift stores that have cost many bucks to get to that stage. *Thrifty*RICHers see half-finished baby afghans, pillows, designer fabrics, and old-fashioned clothing with wonderful pearl buttons as opportunities to complete a creative project with half of the work already finished. New life can be given to clothes with simple changes in length or by adding creative touches. (Remember embroidery to old jeans? It's back!) My friend

Hilda adds bug and butterfly pins to her shoulder. A decorative pin can also be placed over a stubborn stain, if it's in the appropriate place. Many pants can be given minor alterations to fit. I've altered a $5 thrift pair of sans-belt pants in excellent condition ($65 new), and they fit my husband's body just fine. You can also redo a full skirt into a straight one, renew a silk blouse by taking off the out-of-date collar, or revitalize a previous fashion with your own updated touches.

Treasures abound that can be re-gifted

It is surprising how many people donate new or slightly used gifts to thrift stores. Imagine a Waterford vase in the original box from Ireland. Yes. I've seen this. Someone's unwanted gift can be your re-gift for a wedding or anniversary, holiday, or birthday. Many people pass on works of art they do not like (or know the value of). You can give this art new life and a second chance at being appreciated. Pottery can stand alone or can be used to hold other treasures you find. A vase can hold flowers for any occasion and is usually appreciated by the recipient. Someone's creative efforts can be your next gift to an artistic friend or relative. You can re-create your own style, fashion, or home environment with carefully chosen treasures found in thrift stores. Set you own pace and create trends for yourself that others can follow. "Classic" just means it's already been done…and what hasn't? History repeats itself, and things can be renewed, redone, and refreshed. Wow! I found Janet Resnick pottery plates in the Nearly New Thrift Shoppe in Durham. It is hard for me to believe that someone didn't want hand-painted pottery, but that person's recycling became my wonderful treasure.

Share money every month with a cause or causes

Ever since ancient times, the concept of "tithing" or returning 10 percent of your wealth to your community, has been a religious practice. It can be a good practice in and of itself. According to Betty Friedan in *The Fountain of Age* (page 164), for a vital aging we need purpose, projects, and bonds of intimacy. The giving of our time, talents, and money can be our "tithing." Save 10 percent for a rainy day. Giving 5-10 percent to the causes of your choice is a generous goal to share your gratitude.

We give it away to keep it! How very true this is for both our serenity and our resources.

~ Thoughts, Feelings, Actions ~

_____

_____

_____

_____

_____

_____

_____

_____

_____

_____

_____

_____

_____

~ *Thoughts, Feelings, Actions* ~

Thrift store tips

Thrift stores — more than just bargain centers

The mission statement of the Goodwill Community Foundation, a large national chain of thrift stores, is "To provide an environment for people to improve the quality of their lives through employment and learning opportunities with a focus on people with disabilities."

When you buy from GCF and other thrift stores, many operated by nonprofit organizations, the revenues support the organizations' causes, as well as the thrift stores' staff and volunteers.

Another chain of national thrift stores is operated by The Salvation Army. Parent-teacher associations often have thrift stores to augment their schools' finances. Some hospitals, especially university hospitals, have thrift stores mainly staffed by volunteers, and most of their profit supports charitable causes. One of my favorite thrift stores is the Nearly New Thrift Shoppe in Durham, North Carolina. The proceeds help fund scholarships for medical students at Duke University. Habitat for Humanity Thrift Stores help to support the work of that fabulous organization. While refurnishing your own home, the money you spend will be helping to build someone else a home.

Thrift stores for profit and consignment shops are springing up all over the place! I'm very supportive of the owner's entrepreneurial spirit. I frequently contribute to My Secret Closet, started by Cindy and Kim, two sisters in Hillsborough, North Carolina. Every time I prepare for a new season, I'll take a large batch of clothes that no longer fit or that are ready for someone else's enjoyment to consignment shops. Encore and Just Your Style are my favorite clothing consignment shops in Durham. Once and Again and Classic Treasures are home furnishing consignment stores that are marvelous for buying and selling. The consigner receives payment of from 40 percent to 50 percent of the selling price. What could be better? Recycling through consigning also helps support thrift shopping for treasures.

Finding thrift stores

If you are new to thrifting or are new to the area, the place to start your hunt is the local yellow pages under the headings "Thrift" or "Consignment." Goodwill Industries Foundation is also usually listed in the white pages, and it has very consistent and reasonable prices as well as very organized stores. Whether you donate goods or find some great buys that save you money, you are helping others in the community. Where else does finding a great buy do so much good?

Thrift stores in the more upscale parts of the city often have some of the better treasures and are a good place to start. I've also found great items in thrifts in less affluent sections of town. In fact, I've never met a thrift store I didn't like. I've found hidden treasures everywhere including a necklace of top quality lapis beads from a San Francisco Goodwill, a new cashmere sweater from a Junior League Bargain Box in Raleigh, and black walnut tables from a Duke University Salvage thrift store in Durham. In Wichita, Kansas, I found a cloisonne vase ($6.95, but still a deal!). I found a hand-made designer jacket and a silk tunic at a Goodwill store in Ruston, Louisiana. In a San Antonio Goodwill, I found two new pairs of Tencel pants with tags while I was looking for infant clothes for my new grandson. I also scored big time with infant onesies, denim jeans, and many outfits for a dollar each!

Finding those hidden treasures

Every thrift store has hidden treasures. You have to look for them without getting overwhelmed with all the stuff—there is a ton of that. The key is to do a quick swoop to see the big picture and what is available. Then go into areas of interest to you. I have a friend who always goes for the books and finds first editions and current bestsellers, often at $1 each. I've found signed copies of Gloria Steinem books. Some folks go straight for clothes. Some focus on a "collectible" or hobby like glassware, stuffed animals, pottery, jewelry, baskets, or furniture. Again, thrift stores are full of other folk's unfinished projects. So buy up that afghan and put on the border or give it to a knitting friend. At these prices—maybe 25 cents for a skein of cashmere—you can afford to be generous and buy treats for friends and family, just because they would like it!

Stay open to the possibilities

Stay open to the possibilities, even if you have a specific item in mind. You may be looking for black silk pants and find a black bowl perfect as a centerpiece for holding candles or polished stones. I found *Simple Abundance* by Sarah Bain Breathnach, a book that my sister-in-law wanted, while I was looking for black silk pants. I found the silk pants too! There can be something almost mystical about a thrift store experience. When you are open to possibilities, anything is possible. Who knows what treasures and rewards await?

The camaraderie of fellow thrifters

Enjoy the camaraderie of fellow thrifters. Remember, *Thrifty*RICH is about generosity of spirit, spreading the wealth, and sharing the joy. In thrift stores, folks are having a good time because they are spending a little, not a fortune, and wanting others to share the joys of the treasure hunt. I've met women with smaller feet who have handed me a size 5 knowing I could wear it and they could not. We share and laugh and give compliments to each other along the way: "That looks great on you!" It's like a treasure hunt without the competition because my "find" may not suit you, and my treasure may even be your donation. It's all good stuff to someone.

You can find almost anything in a thrift store

You can find almost anything in a thrift store except shelter, gas, and food. Occasionally, you will even find food products, and I have found lamp oil. Most of the furniture in my home is from Goodwill, Habitat for Humanity Thrift Stores, Duke University Salvage, Nearly New Thrift Shoppe, yard sales, and auctions. People give away or leave behind lots of good, barely used stuff.

Clothing in thrifts, especially in wealthy areas, can be amazingly reasonable. How about jeans with a $48 tag for

$3.29? And gift-giving takes on new meaning when you can buy a fabulous present for so little money. How about a basket with scented candles and personalized treats for someone? In the bins, I have found new dish towels, placemats, handkerchiefs, and even new Victoria's Secret silk lingerie.

Thrifting is good therapy

As a group activity or an individual event, shopping the thrifts is a real stress buster. Isn't this fun? What did you find? Look at this! Treasure hunting is as exciting as childhood Easter egg hunts, filling our baskets with brightly colored eggs while experiencing the thrill of the find. Thrifting is like that. The small lacquer box with its design covered with grime polishes up to a rich, shiny glow, perfect for thrift jewelry. The jumble of jewelry with tangled clasps, broken connections, and a slightly rejected look may be your next treasure. A jade bracelet, pearl necklace, or gemstone pin is among the clutter. A cashmere sweater—a tiny hole in neck, easily repaired—may be a $3 hit of the day. And new clothes among the slightly used—gifts for all sizes! Imagine children's clothes, work-out clothes, work clothes, even wedding and cruise clothes at a thrift. You can find them. Didn't we have fun? Look at the things that we found, the laughter that we shared, and the completion of our holiday shopping. And there is the added bonus of our funds supporting the mission of the thrift store. Shopping with a dual purpose!A ThriftyRICH holiday

For holiday and other gift-giving times, use your time and talent in ways that reflect your values. Start your own tradition of recycling gifts or giving from your own stuff, from thrifts, or from yard sales. Holiday gift-making is a great reason to begin a craft you always wanted to learn. Sometimes a gift of your time to perform a household chore or be available to listen, and truly be with someone, is the most thoughtful gift of all.

~ Thoughts, Feelings, Actions ~

_____

_____

_____

_____

_____

_____

_____

_____

_____

_____

_____

_____

_____

_____

_____

_____

_____

_____

*Thrifty*RICH celebrations

Today, as I wonder what to give

Make the holiday season joyful, not burdensome. Do it, make it, and recycle it for personal and inexpensive giving. I discover a honey jar with dipper and think Mary would like that. It's as good as new with fresh honey added. And Angela would like scented dress hangers. My friend and coworker, Terri, gave me an Asian vase, and I was greatly relieved and pleased that she got it from Everything but Grannie's Panties thrift store in Durham. She knew me well enough to know that I don't like new stuff since I can easily get most anything from a thrift store. To me, thrifty-giving is the best way to show one cares.

One of our most memorable Christmases was when we — all 12 in my three-generation family— decided to give only gifts that had a previous life with someone else. My niece and nephew, Lauren and Matthew, went with my sister, Jean, to yard sales. My brother, Brad, discovered a glass double boiler and ancient mung beans in his kitchen cabinet. A red silk dress that had been cycling around the women in the family came back to me. And for lack of anything already used, someone gave recycle bins. Everything but the holiday food was second time around.

Give the gift of time

Living well, enjoying life, having purpose and feeling connected are more about how much of ourselves we can give than how much money we spend or can save. Giving generously of our time, our energy, our talents and our selves does not take money. A handmade card with a future promise of your service—fixing something, sharing an experience, making a meal, or anything the recipient might desire—is a gift from your generous heart and from your talents. A gift of service serves both the recipient and the giver. Both the giver and receiver feel the connection through this exchange, and both are rewarded with a feeling of generosity of spirit. Share your talents, your special gifts, your calm special self.

$\sim$ *Thoughts, Feelings, Actions* $\sim$

_____

_____

_____

_____

_____

_____

_____

_____

_____

_____

_____

_____

All the gifts in the world aren't as special as a note with personal words

A card with a personal note and something that shows you know and care about the person is enough. In fact, all the gifts in the world aren't as special as a note with personal words about the receiver. A handmade card with words of gratitude, praise, and encouragement to the receiver is an excellent gift. Some of my most cherished gifts are from my daughters' hands. I still enjoy some of their early artwork around the house. A construction paper card, when the words are truly personal, can mean so much more than a fancy store-bought card. Hand-made or purchased, it's the personal words that give the meaning to the message.

*A Thrifty*RICH *celebration spa for yourself and friends*

A day of pampering is one way of giving. It's good for you and for your friends. Hold a celebration spa to honor someone on a birthday or other special occasion. Treat your friends to a day of relaxation and healing pleasures. Celebrate their specialness with a delightful event that includes good food—homemade muffins, fresh juice, herbal teas, a simply delicious luncheon of salads and delicious bread, and finally a homemade celebration cake with candles.

Think of activities like a candle-lighting ceremony with well wishes, card-making, stretching and movement with restorative yoga or breathing, healing massage, meditation, and creative visualization. How about a jewelry workshop where everyone adds to a necklace or bracelet for the honoree, and everyone makes earrings to take home? A basket for the honoree full of pampering items is a nice addition. Create your own wish list and think of what you would offer in exchange.

∼ *Thoughts, Feelings, Actions* ∼

A *Thrifty*RICH *Wedding* — *create your own style*

Many weddings these days are about as far removed from the philosophy of *Thrifty*RICH as one can imagine. Much resource is spent on items that do not reflect the deeper values that many couples want to share. Make a list of what is really important for you to express at your wedding: your values, dreams, experiences, and personal talents. Then match the resources you have to those priorities. Create your own style for those "traditional" wedding trimmings. When my daughter, Dona, was planning her wedding, she researched and found that the average wedding cost in her location (Washington, D.C.) was $30,000. My husband and I agreed to give Dona and her fiancé money to do whatever they wished! They chose to use the money for a down payment on their first home and we funded a $2,000 celebration. This is how we did it.

The flowers Purchase huge vases ($10, $15 at thrift stores, big brass). Buy dried flowers—eucalyptus and baby's breath to match the color scheme. On the day of or before the wedding, add huge amounts of fresh flowers from the farmers market or a discount outlet. We used Costco. Ask artistic designer friends or relatives to follow through on pick-up and delivery. Each attendant can carry one long-stemmed flower wrapped in florist tape ($1 for a roll from thrift or hobby store).

The cake Wedding cakes (when they are called wedding cakes) can cost as much as $4-plus per person after cake costs. First thing to do is not to call the cake a "wedding cake." A bakery can stack two or three cakes, and you can add your own flowers (silk or real if you know they are not treated with pesticides). Instead of the tiered cake, try a variety of smaller celebration cakes or ask three friends to each bring their favorite cake. Total cake cost by stacking Whole Food's cakes was around $40. Tiered trays were decorated with homemade cookies and topped with the cakes.

The wedding gown Wedding gowns are way overpriced for what they really are: about $35 worth of fluff. Several options are available to produce the same effect. Thrift or consignment shops sometimes have wedding gowns for $50 or less. If you or a friend or relative can sew, sew it yourself or even see how much it would cost for a seamstress to do it. Materials for wedding gowns can be bought for $5 to $12 a yard at wholesale fabric stores. Even with hand-made lace and hand-woven silk, the cost is usually under $300, total. Rather than have the traditional one piece white wedding gown, think about a mix and match, a beaded top over a full skirt. Many discount stores or thrift stores have tops and skirts that are half off and silk beaded tops for $10. Furthermore, nothing is wrong with borrowing a gown from a friend, renting one, or finding one in the classified ads.

All the above also applies to the dresses for the bridal party.

Veil and crown One of the most precious gifts of my daughter's wedding was a crown handmade by her soon-to-be mother-in-law, Angie Aguayo. It was a work of art with jewels and jewelry pieces provided by family members embedded and sewn into the crown. It looked as if it would sell for thousands—and it probably could have—but the personal sentiment was worth so much more than that.

The photographer Be creative in your plans for having formal and candid photographs and videos of your wedding. You might be surprised at how many friends or family members want to be a part of the picture taking, and the more the merrier. With all of the digital cameras, it is much easier these days to put together a large collage of wedding pictures that guests can then share (over the Internet) and with very little cost. Some of the best joy is in the taking, sorting through, and selecting of the photos, not just in the finished album. My coworker, Edythe, and her husband, David, gave a beautiful and creative gift by compiling the wedding photos in an album. What a gift to treasure forever!

Rental space Use your community or faith facilities. Even if you are not a member of a faith community, you can rent their space reasonably.

Gifts What about gifts for attendants and others who have helped? Use your talents or the talents of others and make or have made special gifts ahead of time—jewelry, pearl necklaces and earrings, whatever your talent can provide. Display each gift in pretty handmade bags to match the color scheme.

Keep the focus on the bride and groom and their celebration with friends and family. You are saving money with a do-it-yourself wedding but do not "do yourself in" trying to do it. Spend the time up front and be available at the time of the event to enjoy and appreciate the now. Pre-plan, delegate, and thank all the relatives and friends who have helped to make the special day a *Thrifty*RICH community wedding.

*Thrifty*RICH Tree

BE

THRIFTYRICH

BE GOOD TO YOURSELF

EXPECT THE UNEXPECTED

BE GRATEFUL, BE GENEROUS

REAP THE BENEFITS OF BENEFITS

RECYCLE, RENEW, REFRESH, AND REDO

MATCH CHOICES WITH RESOURCES, BE RICH

STOP MONEY GOBBLERS, PAY YOURSELF FIRST

DO-IT-YOURSELF, LESSEN COSTS, ENJOY FREEBIES

SAVE AND INVEST MORE THAN 10%, BE FREE OF DEBT

SHARE YOUR RESOURCES, TEACH THE NEXT GENERATION

APPRECIATE ABUNDANCE, ENJOY LIFE'S RICHES, LIVE WELL

INVEST IN THE LONG TERM, COMPARISON SHOP FOR EVERYTHING

THINK THRIFTYRICH:

BE THRIFTYRICH

About the Author

Margie Freeman DeWoskin lives in Durham, North Carolina, with her husband, Rob. She earned her Master's Degree in Social Work with a concentration in gerontology from the University of North Carolina at Chapel Hill. For the past 25 years, Margie has been a counselor, trainer and program director.

For further information regarding speaking engagements, workshops, personal counseling, or purchasing additional copies of the book go to the ThriftyRICH web site at http://home.earthlink.net/~rsdew/ or send an e-mail to margiedew@earthlink.net.

Margie would love to hear from you.